Instant Vortex Air Fryer Oven Mastery

Mouthwatering Recipes and pro Tips To Finally Master Your Instant Vortex Air Fryer Oven With Quick, And Easy To Make Dishes

Martha Brown

© Copyright 2021 - All rights reserved.

Table of Contents

Introduction

One such powerful electric air fryer gives you a massive cooking room that allows you to cook 10-pound chicken, six huge burgers, and more.

For every cooking activity, this electric deep fryer grill rarely uses a lot of oil to make the ideal burgers and juicy, crispy fries with wings; instead, it lets you get 70 percent less calories for all these snacks.

Chapter 1. Air Fryer Guidelines

Air Fryer is a modern innovation among many other kitchen appliances. Although several individuals have already gotten accustomed to the air fryer as one of their favorite kitchen gadgets, several hundred individuals are still unaware of this new technology.

1.1. The Basic Mechanism of Operation

If you are indeed one of the uninformed individuals concerning an air fryer, we will discuss some simple but useful information about an air fryer's mechanism.

Why is Air Fryer outstanding?

It is important to regard an air fryer's cooking process as the unique elements of the gadget. For instance, most of the kitchenware was designed to use the conduction technique to produce foods; while, an air fryer is developed to use Convection – or airflow – for its cooking procedure.

An air fryer will fast and efficiently get your meals completed with a small amount of oil while using Rapid Air Technology.

1.2. The Rapid Air Technology

Don't be surprised to learn that Rapid Air Technology isn't a Tech-material; it's a Tech-procedure instead. Let us explain the operation as quickly as possible.

The air fryer is built to suck air from the setting, and the appliance gets overheated to around 390 degrees Fahrenheit until the machine sucks up enough air. The hot air will then pass into a segmented heating chamber that facilitates the process of cooking.

Simply known as Rapid Air Technology, the mentioned technique stops the use of a significant amount of oil when grilling, cooking, roasting or baking. The process also means that the technique of cooking begins within a very short period.

1.3. Structure of the Air Fryer

As for anyone who will be using the air fryer for the first time, learning about the appliance's components can be very exciting.

<u>An air fryer is made of:</u>

1. Cooking chamber

This chamber is where the entire operation, including making the meal ready, takes place. Although the concept of function remains the same, depending on whether your model is constructed from a single tray or multiple layers of a tray, a cooking chamber's usability may differ.

2. Heating Element

The amount of heat needed to mix up with the moving air is calculated in this part. One of the most cherished virtues of the heating element of an Air Fryer is that it turns off automatically until the appropriate temperature required for cooking has been ascertained – this feature saves power and curbs unnecessary excessive heat.

3. Fan and Grill

This duo works together to ensure that the superheated air is uniformly distributed to the meal. The way the grill is built causes the airflow to be changed, which is

an important component of the entire cooking activity.

4. Exhaust System

This mechanism is designed to help maintain an internal equilibrium pressure and block toxic air from accumulating. With a filter that eliminates the dust and any residual contaminants to clean the exhausted air, you can get some models. There will be no emission of an unwanted odor when doing this.

5. Movable Food Tray

The trays are specifically designed to transfer food that is to be cooked. Some models have a few border walls on the plate, allowing various meals to be cooked simultaneously. You can also get a model of any brand with a universal handle that can be used easily to extract the tray from the heating chamber.

1.4. Benefits of the Air Fryer

Air Fryer Outstanding advantages

- You can prepare healthy fast foods with air fryers better than those cooked with the standard frying technique.

- It's easy to use.

- It needs low maintenance, and washing is easy.

- Over a relatively brief time, the air fryer cooks food.

- In terms of protection, it is safer to use.

Chapter 2: Grill Recipes

1. Island Scallops

Prep + Cook Time: 30-40 minutes | Servings: 4

Ingredients:

- 2 tablespoon Extra Virgin Olive Oil

- 1 1/2-pound sea scallops

- 1 avocado diced

- 15-ounce Pineapple juice

- 1/4 teaspoon salt

- 1/4 teaspoon black pepper

- 1 Red onion diced

- 2 tablespoon rum

- 1/2 cup coconut flakes

- 1/4 cup cilantro

- 3 teaspoon Sea Salt

- 1 papaya diced

- 1 can coconut milk

- 1 lime squeezed

- 2 cup pineapple cubed

Directions:

1. In a large bowl, bring together the pineapple juice, sea salt, coconut milk and rum.

2. In the mixture, soak the sea scallops.

3. Combine and keep the salsa ingredients aside.

4. Assemble skewers that switch between scallops and pieces of pineapple.

5. Place skewers on the holder of the rotisserie.

6. Place it into the Air Fryer Oven. For 10 minutes, set the time. Set the temperature to 400 degrees. Press the button for a rotisserie.

7. Serve with salsa.

2. Shrimp Po' Boy

Prep + Cook Time: 20-40 minutes | Servings: 4

Ingredients:

- 1 large egg, beaten

- 1/4 teaspoon cayenne pepper

- 1 teaspoon Paprika

- 1 cup flour

- 1/2 teaspoon Garlic powder

- 1/2 teaspoon onion powder

- 4 Portuguese rolls

- 16 shrimp, peeled, deveined & tails removed

- 1 cup buttermilk

- 1/2 cup mayonnaise

- 1 teaspoon salt

- 2 tablespoon chili sauce

- 1/2 cup cornmeal

- Dill pickle slices

- Lettuce, shredded

- Tomatoes, sliced

Directions:

1. In a bowl, bring the seasoning ingredients together.

2. Bring together the ingredients for the egg mixture in a second bowl.

3. Bring together the ingredients for the cornmeal mixture in another bowl.

4. To dress the shrimp in the seasoning, whisk the shrimp in the bowl with the seasoning, then dip the shrimp with the egg mixture in the bowl and coat the shrimp cornmeal mixture.

5. On 2 Air Flow Racks, position the shrimp. Sprinkle the shrimp with a spray of olive oil. Place the center and top shelves of the Air Fryer Oven on the racks.

6. Press the power button, raise the cooker's temperature to 390 ° F and reduce the cooking time to 12 minutes. Midway through the cooking time, turn the racks (6 minutes).

7. Mix the ingredients in a bowl with the sauce.

8. Sprinkle the Portuguese rolls with the sauce, then add the lettuce, tomatoes and pickles to the rolls.

9. Topple the shrimp with the rolls.

3. Turkey Guacamole Burger

Prep + Cook Time: 40-50 minutes | Servings: 4

Ingredients:

- 1¾ teaspoon salt

- 1 jalapeno, seeded & minced

- 2 avocados, crushed

- 1/4 cup margarine

- 1/2 small red onion, chopped finely

- 2 tablespoon cilantros, chopped

- 2 tablespoon breadcrumbs, plain

- 1/2 cup queso fresco, crumbled

- 1/2 cup diced canned tomatoes, liquid drained

- 1/2 plum tomato, diced small

- 2 teaspoon Lime juice

- 1 pound ground turkey

- 2 teaspoon cilantros, chopped

- 4 hamburger buns

Directions:

1. Mix the ingredients for the burger in a bowl. Shape the mixed ingredients into four burgers.

2. In a different bowl, toss the guacamole ingredients until it becomes creamy.

3. Place an Air Flow Rack for the patties. Place the rack on the Power Air Fryer oven's middle rack.

4. Press the power button to raise the cooking temperature to 390 ° F and cook for 20 minutes.

5. Flip patties halfway through cooking time (10 minutes). Set the hamburgers aside.

6. Cut the buns of the hamburger horizontally in half and spread with the margarine.

7. On an Air Flow Rack, position 2 buns. Place the rack on the Power Air Fryer oven's middle rack.

8. Press and cook with the power button until the rolls are golden brown (about 3 minutes). Repeat until it is toasted with all the buns.

9. With the guacamole and queso fresco, place the burgers on the buns.

Chapter 3. Breakfast Recipes

4. Green Tomato BLT

Prep + Cook Time: 35 minutes | Servings: 4

<u>Ingredients:</u>

- 2 medium green tomatoes (about 10 oz.)

- ¼ tsp pepper

- ½ tsp salt

- 1 cup panko (Japanese) bread crumbs

- ¼ cup all-purpose flour

- 1 large egg, beaten

- 2 green onions, finely chopped

- 1 tsp snipped fresh dill or ¼ tsp dill weed

- ½ cup reduced-fat mayonnaise

- 8 slices whole wheat bread, toasted

- 8 cooked center-cut bacon strips

- 4 Bibb or Boston lettuce leaves

Directions:

1. Ensure the air fryer is preheated to 350-degree F and sprinkle some cooking spray on the basket.

2. Create eight slices, each slice 1/4 inch thick, of your tomato. Finally, brush the tomato slices with salt and pepper.

3. Get three separate shallow bowls and put each one with the bread, flour, and egg. Dip the tomato slices in the starch, then shake in the egg and eventually the crumb mixture to eliminate the excess. The slices can be divided into batches.In the air fryer basket, place the tomato slices to form a single plate, then spray with cooking spray.Enable around 8-12 minutes to cook, turn halfway, and sprinkle with extra cooking spray. Remove to remain warm until the golden-brown hue is consistent. For the other slices of tomato, do the same.Create a combination of the green onions, dill, and mayonnaise before frying the tomato slices. Lay two bacon strips, one cabbage, and two tomato slices on each of the four slices of bread. Then spread the mixture of mayonnaise over the remaining bread slices, and put it over the end.

Immediately serve.

5. Egg Rolls

Prep + Cook Time: 50 minutes | Servings: 16

Ingredients:

- 1 (4 oz.) can dice green chiles, drained

- 4 green onions, sliced

- 1 cup sharp Cheddar cheese, shredded

- 1½ cups shredded jalapeno Jack cheese

- 1 (13.5 oz.) can make spinach, drained

- 2 cups frozen corn, thawed

- 1 (15 oz.) can black beans, drained and rinsed

- 1 tsp salt

- 1 tsp ground cumin

- 1 tsp chili powder

- 1 (16 oz.) package egg roll wrappers

- Cooking spray

Directions:

1. In a large mixing bowl, combine the green chiles, cheddar cheese, green onions, jalapeno cheese, spinach, maize, beans, cumin, salt, and chili powder to act as a filling.

2. Lay the wrapping of an egg roll at an angle and use your finger to gently moisten the four sides with water.

3. Divide the filling into four and apply the middle of the wrapper to each half. Over the filling, fold one corner and tuck in the sides, making a roll. Although applying some cooking spray to mist the roll, do the same with the other wrappers.

4. Make sure the air fryer is preheated to 390-degree F.

5. Move the egg rolls to the basket while leaving some room and, if necessary, cook them in batches.

6. Enable the egg rolls to fry for 8 minutes, then flip and cook for an additional 4 minutes or until the skin is crispy.

6. Breakfast Frittata

Prep + Cook Time: 40 minutes | Servings: 2

Ingredients:

- 1 pinch cayenne pepper (optional)

- 1 green onion, chopped

- 2 tbsp. red bell pepper, diced

- ¼ lb. breakfast sausage, fully cooked and crumbled

- 4 eggs, lightly beaten

- ½ cup shredded Cheddar-Monterey Jack cheese blend

- Cooking spray

Directions:

1. Make a combination of cayenne, tomato, bell pepper, bacon, eggs, and Cheddar-Monterey Jack Cheese to make a clean bowl.

2. Make sure the air fryer is preheated to 360-degree F. Get a 6x2-inch cake pan that can suit with a little cooking spray into the air fryer to spray the same.

3. Transfer the egg mixture to the tray that has been sprayed.

4. Enable it to cook the mixture until it is ready. It takes up to 18 or 20 minutes to complete.

7. Spinach Frittata

Prep + Cook Time: 15 minutes | Servings: 2

Ingredients:

- 1 small red onion, minced

- 1/3 pack of spinach

- 3 eggs, whisked

- Salt and ground black pepper to taste

- Mozzarella cheese

Directions:

1. Make sure the air fryer is preheated to 360-degree F.Before adding the minced onions, keep the oil in the baking pan for a minute. Enable the onions to live for another 2-3 minutes or before they become translucent.Spinach is added and fried until half-cooked (for about 3-5 minutes). If the spinach looks dry, do not fret, just continue frying. The whisked eggs are seasoned, and cheese added.Finally, pour in the pan the seasoned mixture and bake until cooked-it takes roughly 8 minutes.

8. Breakfast Soufflé

Prep + Cook Time: 25 minutes | Servings: 2

<u>Ingredients:</u>

- Red chili pepper

- Parsley

- 2 eggs, beaten

- 2 tbsp. cream (light)

<u>Directions:</u>

1. Chop your parsley and chili into fine pieces.

2. Place the eggs, alongside the parsley, cream, and pepper, in a bowl, stir.

3. Pour the mixture of eggs into the dishes until they are half-filled. Allow it to bake at 390-degree F for 8 minutes.

4. Cook for only 5 minutes, if you prefer the Souffles Bayeux soft.

Chapter 4. Fast Food Recipes

9. Five Cheese Pull-Apart Bread

Prep + Cook Time: 20 minutes | Servings: 2

Ingredients:

- 1 oz. goats Cheese

- 1 oz. Cheddar Cheese

- 1 oz. Moz.zarella Cheese

- 1 oz. Edam cheese

- 1 oz. soft cheese

- 4 oz. butter

- Salt and ground black pepper to taste

- 2 tsp chives

- 2 tsp garlic puree

- 1 large bread loaf

Directions:

1. It's indeed necessary to grate the hard cheese into four separate piles and set it aside.

2. Place it on medium heat and get a clean saucepan. In a saucepan, heat the butter and whisk in the pepper, cinnamon, chives and garlic. Enable the mixture to cook while mixing for another 2 minutes. Only put aside.

3. Use a sharp bread knife to make little slits in the bread. Until each slit is well covered, cover each whole slit with garlic butter. To guarantee the lovely smooth flavor at the top, fill all the slits with soft cheese.

4. In any other slit, add a little goat's cheese and a little cheddar.

5. To those that have not been filled, add the Edam and Mozzarella.

6. Transfer to the air fryer and allow to cook at 360-degree F for 4 minutes or until the cheese and warm bread are melted.

7. Just serve.

10. Air Fryer Grilled Cheese

Prep + Cook Time: 12 minutes | Servings: 1

Ingredients:

- 2 slices of bread I used GF bread

- Butter

- 1 slice of cheese

Directions:

1. Add butter generously to one side of each of the slices of bread; however, avoid too much butter.

2. Add the folded cheese in-between the bread slices while ensuring that the buttered side is facing out. Avoid letting the cheese hang outside the bread; otherwise, it will burn in the air fryer.

3. If you want to grill, set the air fryer temperature to 360-degree F and the timer to 8 minutes.

4. Flip the bread after 5 minutes.

5. Allow to cool and serve.

Chapter 5. Appetizers and Snack Recipes

11. British Fish and Chip Shop Healthy Battered Sausage and Chips

Prep + Cook Time: 45 minutes | Servings: 2

<u>Ingredients:</u>

- 2 large potatoes, peeled

- 1 tbsp. olive oil

- 2 slices whole meal bread

- Salt and ground black pepper to taste

- 1 medium egg beaten

- 4 oz. plain flour

- 4 medium-thick sausages

<u>Directions:</u>

1. Make sure the air fryer is preheated to 360-degree F.

2. Cut the peeled potatoes into chips, place them in the fryer and apply a spoonful of olive oil.

3. By transferring the whole whole meal bread into the air fryer, right on the chips, prepare your breaded crust and harden it for about 5 minutes. After 5 minutes, cut the bread and split it into bread crumbs.

4. Combine, in a clean bowl, the breadcrumbs with some salt and pepper. Take a separate dish and add the egg. Then apply the flour to the third dish.

5. By placing each sausage in your hand and rolling it into the flour, the egg, and finally, in the mixture of bread crumbs, make the breaded sausage.

6. For all the bits of sausage or at least four pounded sausages, repeat.

7. Transfer the battered sausages, on top of the potatoes, into an air fryer.

8. Allow it to cook at 360-degree F for 10 minutes. After 10 minutes, cut the chips and only cook the sausages for an additional 5 minutes.

9. Just serve.

12. Pigs in a Blanket

Prep + Cook Time: 25 minutes | Servings: 16

Ingredients:

- 1 can (8 oz.) of crescent rolls

- 1 pack (12 oz.) of cocktail franks or mini smoked sausages

Directions:

The cocktail franks are removed and removed from the package. Dry with a paper towel to get rid of the residual moisture.

Remove the dough from the can of crescent rolls and make eight triangles out of it. Render each of the eight triangles two thin triangles. Ultimately, you'll have 16 triangles.Place one frank (on the widest part) on the triangle and roll up. Do the same for the other triangles and franks. Transfer about 8 'Pigs in a Blanket' to the basket of the air fryer and fry at 330 F for 8 minutes. Do the same for the remaining eight.

Serve alongside spicy ketchup, gesso dip, salsa, or mustard, the fried Pigs in a Blanket.

13. Healthy Flapjacks Recipe

Prep + Cook Time: 20 minutes | Servings: 4

Ingredients:

- 4 oz. butter

- 10 oz. gluten-free oats

- 4 oz. brown sugar

- 2 tbsp. honey

Directions:

1. On top of the air fryer grill plate, place the baking pan and ensure that it slots inside the air fryer in place.

2. Dice the butter into quarters and transfer it to the baking tray to transfer them. Enable it to cook at 360-degree F degree for 2 minutes or until the butter is melted.

3. In the mixer, mix the gluten-free oats until they look like breadcrumbs.

4. Combine the honey and brown sugar, and then the oats. When you have a smooth blend, mix well with a fork.

5. Allow them to cook at 320-degree F for 10 minutes.

6. Raise the temperature to 360-degree F and give an additional 5 minutes to cook.

7. Remove and serve.

14. Air Fryer Chewy Granola Bars

Prep + Cook Time: 20 minutes | Servings: 6

Ingredients:

- 10 oz. gluten-free oats

- 1 oz. brown sugar

- 1 tsp vanilla essence

- 1 tsp cinnamon

- 1 tbsp. olive oil

- 3 tbsp. honey

- 2 oz. melted butter

- 1 medium apple, peeled and cooked

- Handful raisins

Directions:

1. After blending the gluten-free oats into a smooth mixture, toss in the other dry ingredients.

2. Combine the wet ingredients into the baking pan of the air fryer. Stir well using a small wooden spoon.

3. Transfer the dry ingredients from the blender into the baking pan. Mix thoroughly with a fork.

4. Toss in the raisins and press down the mixture into the baking pan until it is all level.

5. Allow cooking for 10 minutes at 320-degree F.

6. Raise the temperature to 360-degree F and cook for an extra 5 minutes.

7. Remove and transfer into the freezer for about 5 minutes or until it stiffens up.

8. Cut into chewy sizes.

9. Serve your granola bars.

15. Roasted Corn

Prep + Cook Time: 25 minutes | Servings: 2-3

Ingredients:

- 4 fresh ears of corn

- 2 to 3 tsp vegetable oil

- Salt and ground black pepper to taste

Directions:

1. Wash them and pat them dry after getting rid of the husks of grain. If it was too small for your basket of maize, you'd have to cut it.

2. Cover the corn with a few drizzles of vegetable oil before the oil coats the corn well.

3. To season it to taste, add some salt and pepper.

4. Allow it to cook at 400-degree F for 10 minutes.

Chapter 6. Chicken and Turkey Recipes

16. Thai Peanut Chicken Egg Rolls

Prep + Cook Time: 20 minutes | Servings: 3-4

Ingredients:

- 2 cups rotisserie chicken, shredded

- ¼ cup Thai peanut sauce

- 4 egg roll wrappers

- 1 medium carrot, very thinly sliced or ribboned

- ¼ red bell pepper, julienned

- 3 green onions, chopped

- Non-stick cooking spray or sesame oil

Directions:

1. Ensure that your air fryer is preheated to 390-degree F.

2. Get a small bowl and place the chicken in it alongside the Thai peanut sauce.

3. With the egg roll wrappers laid out on a clean, dry surface, arrange ¼ carrot, bell pepper, and onions to accommodate the bottom third of the egg roll wrapper.

4. Spread ½ cup of the chicken mixture over the vegetables.

5. Using water, moisten the outer edges of the wrapper. Roll the wrapper tightly by folding the sides of the wrapper towards the center.

6. Do the same for the other wrappers (pending this time, cover them with a damp paper towel).

7. Using a non-stick cooking spray, spread both sides of the assembled egg rolls well.

8. Transfer the sprayed egg rolls into your air fryer. Bake for 6-8 minutes at 390-degree F or until you have a crispy and golden-brown appearance.

9. Slice the baked chicken in half and serve with extra Thai Peanut Sauce for dipping.

17. Friendly Air fryer Whole Chicken

Prep + Cook Time: 45 minutes | Servings: 4

Ingredients:

- Medium whole chicken (about 3 lbs.)

- Salt and ground black pepper to taste

- 1 tbsp. mixed herbs

- 1 tbsp. olive oil

- 1 large onion

Directions:

Ensure that your air fryer is preheated to 340-degree F. To the skin of your nice and dry chicken, sprinkle salt, pepper, and mixed herbs, before rubbing olive oil. Take away the giblets present in the chicken. Without removing the skin of the onion, chop it in half and place it in the chicken's cavity. Transfer the chicken into the air fryer upside down and with the bottom stuck in the air. Allow cooking for 20 minutes before turning it over. This time around, the breast faces up. Cook for another 20 minutes. Remove and serve warm.

18. KFC Chicken in the Air Fryer

Prep + Cook Time: 30 minutes | Servings: 4

Ingredients:

- 1 whole chicken

- 1 oz. KFC spice blend

- 10 oz. bread crumbs

- 4 oz. plain flour

- 3 small eggs beaten

Directions:

1. After chopping your chicken into pieces of desired sizes, set them aside.

2. You may separate the wings, things, drumsticks, and breast, or have the wings and the breast together.

3. Get a clean bowl, and make a mixture of the KFC spice and breadcrumbs.

4. Get another clean bowl and place your flour.

5. In a third clean bowl, place your beaten eggs.

6. After rolling the chicken pieces in the flour, roll it in the egg, and finally in the spicy breadcrumbs.

7. Set your air fryer to 360-degree F and cook the rolled chicken for 18 minutes. Do not withdraw until it is well cooked in the middle.

8. Serve.

19. KFC Easy Chicken Strips in the Air Fryer

Prep + Cook Time: 25 minutes | Servings: 2

Ingredients:

- 1 chicken breast, chopped into strips

- Salt and ground black pepper to taste

- 3 oz. bread crumbs

- ½ oz. plain oats

- ½ oz. desiccated coconut

- ¼ oz. KFC spice blend get our recipe here

- 2 oz. plain flour

- 1 small egg, beaten

Directions:

1. Make strips out of your chicken breast.

2. Get a clean bowl, and make a mixture of salt, pepper, breadcrumbs, oats, coconut, and the KFC spice blend.

3. Get another clean bowl and place your egg.

4. In the third clean bowl, add your plain flour.

5. Dip the strips in the plain flour first, before the egg, and finally, the spicy layer.

6. Set your Air Fryer to 360-degree F and cook the dipped chicken for eight minutes.

7. Reduce the temperature to 320-degree F and cook for an extra four minutes to ensure that the chicken cooks well in the middle.

8. Serve.

20. KFC Popcorn Chicken in the Air Fryer

Prep + Cook Time: 25 minutes | Servings: 2

Ingredients:

- 1 chicken breast

- 2 oz. plain flour

- 1 small egg, beaten

- Salt and ground black pepper to taste

- 2 oz. bread crumbs

- ¼ oz. KFC spice blend get the recipe here

Directions:

1. Blend your chicken in your food processor until you have something like a minced chicken.

2. Create your factory line – the first bowl containing your flour; the second containing your beaten egg; and the third containing a mixture of salt, pepper, bread crumbs, and finally, the KFC spice blend.

3. Like another factory line, transform the minced chicken into balls.

4. Roll the balls in the flour first, then in the egg, and finally in the spiced breadcrumbs.

5. Transfer the rolled chicken balls into the air fryer. Set it to 360-degree F and cook for about 10 to 12 minutes, or until you are sure the chicken is well cooked in the middle.

21. Everything Bagel Chicken Strips

Prep + Cook Time: 25 minutes | Servings: 4

Ingredients:

- 1 day-old everything bagel, torn

- ½ cup panko bread crumbs

- ½ cup grated parmesan cheese

- ¼ tsp red pepper flakes, crushed

- 1 lb. chicken tenderloins

- ½ tsp salt

- ¼ cup butter, cubed

Directions:

1. Ensure that your Air Fryer is preheated to 400-degree F.

2. Pulse the torn bagel in a food processor and withdraw only when you have coarse crumbs. Separate ½ of the cup bagel crumbs and transfer it into a shallow bowl, mix it with panko, cheese, and pepper flakes. You may retain or discard the other half of the bagel crumbs.

3. Get a shallow bowl that is safe for use in a microwave, heat microwave butter until it melts.

4. Sprinkle your chicken with salt and dip it in warm butter before coating it with a crumb mixture. You may pat the chicken to ensure it retains the crumb.

5. After spraying the air fryer basket with cooking spray, transfer the chicken to form a single layer in the basket.

6. You may divide the chicken into batches. Cook each batch for seven minutes before turning it over to the other side. Cook until the pink appearance of the chicken is replaced by the golden-brown coating (for about seven to eight minutes).

7. Serve immediately.

Chapter 7. Lamb Recipes

22. Meatballs with Feta

Prep + Cook Time: 20 minutes | Servings: 10

Ingredients:

- 6 oz. lamb mince or lean minced beef

- 1 slice of stale white bread, turned into fine crumbs

- ½ tbsp. lemon peel, grated

- 1 tbsp. fresh oregano, finely chopped

- 2 oz. Greek feta, crumbled

- Freshly ground black pepper

- Round, shallow Air Fryer dish, 6 - inch

- Tapas forks

Directions:

1. Ensure that you have preheated your Air Fryer to 390-degree F.

2. Create a combination of mince, breadcrumbs, lemon peel, oregano, feta, and black pepper and knead it all together in a dish.

54

3. Out of the combination, create ten equivalent parts. Making ten smooth balls out of the 10 portions with your wet palms.

4. Into the oven dish, move the balls and then into the basket.

5. Put the basket in the fryer and allow 8 minutes to bake. When they are nicely orange, the balls are full.

6. In addition to tapas forks, eat when hot in a bowl.

Chapter 8. Beef Recipes

23. Beef Wellington (medium rear)

Prep + Cook Time: 55 minutes | Servings: 4

Ingredients:

- 2 lb. beef fillet

- Salt and ground black pepper to taste

- Homemade short crust pastry

- Homemade chicken liver pate

- 1 medium egg, beaten

Directions:

1. Clean out your beef fillet, remove any visible fat, and season with pepper and salt. Then seal it up using cling film and fridge it for an hour.

2. Create your homemade short crust pastry and your chicken liver pate.

3. With your short crust pastry rolled out, use your pastry brush to coat all around the edges with a beaten egg. This ensures that it is sticky for sealing.

4. Right inside the outer egg line, place a thin layer of the homemade pate until the white pastry is no longer visible.

5. Remove the cling film from the meat and put the meat in the middle, on the top, of the pate and apply a little force to push it down a bit.

7. Seal the pastry around the pate and the meat.

8. Ensure that you score at the top of the pastry to ensure that the meat is not entirely devoid of air.

9. Transfer into the grill plan of the air fryer.

10. Allow cooking for 35 minutes at 320-degree F.

11. Remove after 35 minutes and allow to rest for some minutes.

12. Slice and serve alongside roast potatoes.

24. Garlic Butter Steak with Herbs

Prep + Cook Time: 30 minutes | Servings: 2

Ingredients:

- 2 cloves garlic, minced

- 4 tablespoons butter

- 1 teaspoon chives, chopped

- 2 teaspoons parsley, chopped

- 1 teaspoon rosemary, chopped

- 1 teaspoon thyme, chopped

- 2 rib eye steaks

- Salt and pepper to taste

Directions:

1. Combine the garlic, butter and herbs in a bowl.

2. Refrigerate for 20 minutes.

3. Roll the butter mixture into a log.

4. Sprinkle both sides of steaks with salt and pepper.

5. Set air fryer to grill.

6. Air fry at 400 degrees F for 15 minutes, flipping once or twice.

7. Slice the herb butter.

8. Top the steaks with herb butter.

Chapter 9. Pork Recipes

25. Sticky BBQ Pork Strips

Prep + Cook Time: 25 minutes | Servings: 4-6

Ingredients:

- 6 pcs pork loin chops

- Freshly ground pepper

- 2 tbsp. honey

- 2 tbsp. soy sauce

- 1 tsp balsamic vinegar

- ¼ tsp ground ginger (or ½ tsp freshly grated ginger)

- 1 garlic clove, chopped

Directions:

1. Ensure that the Air Fryer is preheated to 400-degree F.

2. To spray the air-fryer basket by using cooking spray.

3. Take a shallow cup and mix the eggs and milk in it together.

4. Get another shallow bowl and put the pecans alongside the breadcrumbs.

5. Coat the pork chops with flour and shake to remove the excess flour.

6. Onto mixture of the egg and the crumb mixture, dip the coated pork chops. Pat will occasionally ensure that the blends do not slip off. You should work in batches if you have lots of pork chops.

7. Place the chops into a single sheet in the air fryer basket and lightly spray with the cooking spray.

8. Allow the pork chops to cook inside the air fryer for 12 to 15 minutes or until they become golden brown. After 6-7 minutes, turn the chops and spray gently again.

9. After cooking, depart and keep warm. Then cook the other chops.

10. While boiling, place the unused ingredients in a small saucepan and boil until the mixture is slightly thickened while stirring. This should, at maximum, take 6 to 8 minutes.

11. Serve the chops with butter.

Chapter 10. Fish Recipes

26. Sesame Seeds Fish Fillet

Prep + Cook Time: 40 minutes | Servings: 3-5

Ingredients:

- 5 frozen fish fillets (if it's not frozen, just cut the cooking time by roughly 3 minutes)

- 3 tbsp. plain flour

- 1 egg, beaten

Coating:

- A handful of sesame seeds

- 3 tbsp. oil

- Pinch of ground black pepper

- Pinch of sea salt

- 5-6 soda biscuit crumbs (or any plain biscuits you have or breadcrumbs)

- Pinch of rosemary herbs, optional

Directions:

Coating

Without adding oil to the pan, fry the sesame seed in it for 2 minutes while stirring consistently. Once they become brown, remove them from the pan.

Get a large plate and make a mixture of all the coating ingredients.

Fish Fillet

1. Ensure that your Air Fryer is preheated to 360-degree F and lined with aluminum foil.

2. Proceed to arrange your ingredients to ensure efficiency following the order below.

3. Dip the fish in the flour, then the egg, and finally in the coating mixture.

3. Place the coated fish inside the air fryer.

4. Cook for 10 minutes if it's frozen fillet, flip the fish and cook for extra 4 minutes.

5. If the fillet is not frozen, cook the first side for 8 minutes and the second for 2 minutes Serve!

27. Thai Fish Cakes with Mango Salsa

Prep + Cook Time: 35 minutes | Servings: 4

Ingredients:

- 1 ripe mango, peeled

- 3 tbsp. fresh coriander or flat-leaf parsley

- 1½ tsp red chili paste

- Juice and zest of 1 lime

- 1 lb. white fish fillet (pollack, cod, pangasius, tilapia)

- 1 egg, beaten

- 1 green onion, finely chopped

- 2 oz. ground coconut

Directions:

1. Make sure that your Air Fryer is preheated to 375-degree F.

2. Cut the peeled mangoes into small cubes and blend them together with a tablespoon of coriander, 1/2 teaspoon of red chili paste, juice and half a lime zest in a cup.

3. Purée the fish and apply one shell, one teaspoon of salt, and the remaining lime zest, red chili paste, and lime juice to the food processor. Mix these with the remaining coriander, 2 tablespoons of coconut, and the green onion.

4. Get a clean plate of soup and move the rest of the coconut into this one. Out of the fish mixture, make 12 portions, with each part made into round cakes. Finally, coat the coconut with each cake,

5. In your air fryer basket, arrange six fish cakes and fry the fish cakes for about 7 minutes, or until the golden-brown color is visible. For the other fish cakes, do the same.

6. Take the fried cakes from the fish and serve with the mango salsa. Pandan rice and stir-fried pak choi can also be mixed with it.

.

Chapter 11. Seafood Recipes

28. Cod Pie with Palmit

Prep + Cook Time: 45 minutes | Servings: 4-6

Ingredients:

- 2 ¼ lb. cod

- 4 ½ lb. of natural heart previously grated and cooked

- 12 eggs

- 1 ½ cup olive oil

- 7 oz. of olives

- Tomato Chopped garlic, paprika and sliced onion

- Green seasoning

Directions:

1. In a frying pan, cook the cod and, after cooking, destroy it.

2. Drain the heart of the palm well on the reservation.

3. Along with tomatoes, garlic, paprika, ginger, green seasoning and half of the pitted olives, sauté the cod and palm hearts in olive oil for 20 minutes.

4. Pour 6 eggs into the sample and stir for 5 minutes.

5. Grease the olive oil trays and place the mixture into them.

6. Beat the rest of the eggs and spill over the top evenly.

7. Add tomatoes and olives to garnish.

8. Bake for 40 minutes in the air-fryer at 380 F.

29. Roasted Hake with Coconut Milk

Prep + Cook Time: 25 minutes | Servings: 4-6

Ingredients:

- 2 ¼ lb. hake fillet

- ½ lb. sliced mozzarella

- 1 can of sour cream

- 1 bottle of coconut milk

- 1 onion

- 1 tomato

- Salt and black pepper to taste.

- Lemon juice

Directions:

1. With salt, pepper and lemon, season the fillets.

2. Let them stand for ten minutes.

3. Arrange the fillets and put each one in the center of the mozzarella slices and roll it up like a fillet.

4. The fillets were rolled up after all.

5. Just get a tray.

6. Place on top of the tomato and onion slices (sliced).

7. Attach the sour cream and coconut milk mixture to the top.

8. Bake for 20 minutes inside an air-fryer at 400-degree F, coated with aluminum foil.

9. Then, to finish baking, remove it.

Chapter 12. Home Bakery Recipes

30. Rich Fruit Scones

Prep + Cook Time: 15 minutes | Servings: 4

Ingredients:

- 0.5 lb. self-rising flour

- 2 oz. butter

- 2 oz. sultanas

- 1 oz. caster sugar

- 1 medium egg

- Milk

Directions:

1. Place the flour and butter in a clean mixing bowl and rub the fat into the flour.

2. The sultanas are added, followed by the caster sugar and the egg is gradually split into the mixture.

3. Until you have a consistent blend, mix thoroughly with a teaspoon.

4. When you have a smooth scone dough, add a little milk intermittently.

5. Shape into scones with the dough.

6. Move the scones into the air-fryer grill tray.

7. Enable it to cook for 8 minutes at 360-degree F.

8. Remove and serve warm.

Chapter 13. Rice Recipes

31. Sticky Mushroom Rice

Prep + Cook Time: 25 minutes | Servings: 6

Ingredients:

- 16 oz. jasmine rice, uncooked

- 4 tbsp. maple syrup

- 2 tsp Chinese 5 Spice

- 4 tbsp. rice vinegar or white wine

- ½ cup soy sauce, you can use gluten-free tamari

- ½ tsp ground ginger

- 4 cloves garlic, finely chopped

- 16 oz. Cremini mushrooms wiped clean (any other mushrooms cut in half)

- ½ cup peas, frozen

Directions:

1. Store your cooked rice separately.

2. Combine the maple syrup, rice vinegar, soy sauce, ground ginger, garlic, and 5 Chinese spices in a clean dish.

3. Make sure the air fryer is preheated to 350-degree F.

4. In an air fryer, cause the mushrooms to cook for 10 minutes.

5. Open an air fryer after 10 minutes and shake or stir the mushrooms.

6. Pour the liquid mixture over the mushrooms that have been roasted, followed by the peas.

7. Stir and boil for an additional 5 minutes.

8. Finally, add the cooked hot rice to the mushroom sauce and stir well.

9. Serve.

.

Chapter 14. Beans and Legumes Recipes

32. Falafel

Prep + Cook Time: 1 d 1 h 45 m | Servings: 15

Ingredients:

- 1 cup dry garbanzo beans

- 1 clove garlic

- 1 small red onion, quartered

- 3/4 cup fresh flat-leafed parsley, stems removed

- 1 ½ cups fresh cilantro, stems removed

- 1 tbsp. ground cumin

- 1 tbsp. Sriracha sauce

- 2 tbsp. chickpea flour

- 1 tbsp. ground coriander

- Salt and ground black pepper to taste

- ¼ tsp baking soda

- ½ tsp baking powder

- Cooking spray

Directions:

1. Loosen and remove the skin after soaking the chickpeas in water for 24 hours by rubbing them with your fingertips. The skin-less chickpeas are rinsed and drained, and spread on a big, clean dish towel. This will cause them to dry up.

2. In a food processor, mix the garlic, onion, parsley, cilantro and chickpeas and blend until you have a rough paste. In a large bowl, pour the mixture into it.

3. Toss the cumin, Sriracha salt, chickpea flour, coriander, salt and pepper into the bowl containing the blended mixture. Before covering the mug, combine thoroughly. For 1 hour, let the mixture rest.

4. Ensure your air fryer is preheated to 375-degree F.

5. Before thoroughly mixing with your hands to ensure even blending, apply baking soda and baking powder to the chickpea mixture. Mold the mixture into 15 equal-sized balls, softly pressing each ball to create patties. With cooking sauce, spray the patties.

6. Arrange seven falafel patties in the basket of the air fryer and give 10 minutes to cook.

7. Remove the cooked falafel and place them on a plate.

8. Do the same for the other eight falafels, cooking for 10-12 minutes

Chapter 15. Pasta Recipes

33. Maccaroni and Cheese Mini Quiche Recipe

Prep + Cook Time: 30 minutes | Servings: 4

<u>**Ingredients:**</u>

- Shortcrust pastry

- 1 tsp garlic puree

- 2 tbsp. Greek yogurt

- 8 tbsp. leftover macaroni and cheese

- 2 large eggs, beaten

- 12 oz. whole milk

- Grated cheese, optional

<u>**Directions:**</u>

1. Rub the bottom with some flour when washing your ramekin.

2. On the bottom of the ramekin, pass the short crust pastry.

3. Get a small, clean bowl and mix the garlic, Greek yogurt and the unused macaroni in it.

4. Cover the ramekins (up to 3/4 full) with the yogurt and garlic mixture.

5. Grab a separate bowl and combine the milk and eggs. Pour the paste over the cheese with the macaroni.

6. Make sure the air fryer is preheated to 355-degree F.

7. Load the cheese onto the ramekins as toppings and pass them to the air fryer.

8. Enable them to cook for 20 minutes.

9. Remove and serve.

Chapter 16. Potato Recipes

34. Skin on French Fries

Prep + Cook Time: 20 minutes | Servings: 2

Ingredients:

- 2 large white potatoes

- 1 tsp olive oil

- 2 tsp chives, dried

- Salt and ground black pepper to taste

Directions:

1. While scrubbing the potatoes, get rid of any eyes.

2. Slice the washed potatoes into French fries and transfer the same into a bowl.

3. Add the olive oil and the entire seasoning in the bowl and mix well with your hands.

4. Transfer the coated slices into the air fryer basket, and allow cooking for 15 minutes at 360-degree F.

5. Shake after 7 or 8 minutes.

6. After 15 minutes, withdraw the fries and serve alongside mayonnaise or ketchup.

35. Hash Brown Recipe

Prep + Cook Time: 35 minutes | Servings: 8

Ingredients:

- 4 large potatoes, peeled and finely grated

- 2 tsp vegetable oil

- 2 tsp chili flakes

- 1 tsp onion powder, optional

- 1 tsp garlic powder, optional

- Ground black pepper to taste

- Salt to taste

- 2 tbsp. corn flour

Directions:

1. After the shredded potatoes have been soaked in cold water, drain the water and repeat the step to get rid of excess starch from the potatoes.

2. Get a non-stick pan, and in it, heat one teaspoon of vegetable oil. Sauté the shredded potatoes until they are cooked slightly – it takes about 3 or 4 minutes.

3. Allow the potatoes to cool down before transferring them to a plate.

4. Combine chili flakes, onion powder, garlic, pepper, salt, and corn flour and mix thoroughly.

5. Spread the mixture over the potatoes plate and pat firmly using the fingers.

6. Keep in the fridge for 20 minutes.

7. Ensure that your air fryer is preheated to 360-degree F.

8. Remove the refrigerated potato and halve it into pieces using a knife.

9. Using some oil, brush the wire basket of the air fryer gently.

10. Transfer the hash brown pieces of potatoes into the basket and allow to air-dry for 15 minutes at 360-degree F.

11. Remove the basket and turn the hash browns to the other side after 6 minutes. This ensures even frying.

12. Serve while hot alongside ketchup.

Chapter 17. Vegetables

36. Asparagus Fries

Prep + Cook Time: 25 minutes | Servings: 6

Ingredients:

- 1 large egg, beaten

- 1 tsp honey

- ½ cup Parmesan cheese, grated

- 1 cup panko bread crumbs

- 12 asparagus spears, trimmed

- 1 pinch cayenne pepper, optional

- ¼ cup Greek yogurt

- ¼ cup stone-ground mustard

Directions:

1. Ensure that your air fryer is preheated to 400-degree F.

2. Get a long, narrow dish, and in it combing egg and honey. Beat together and set aside.

3. On a separate plate, combine the Parmesan cheese and panko.

4. After coating each asparagus stalk in the egg mixture, roll it also in the panko mix and allow thorough coating.

5. Arrange six spears in the air fryer and allow cooking to the desired brownness – this takes 4 to 6 minutes. Do the same for the other spears.

6. Get a small bowl, and in it, mix the cayenne pepper, yogurt, and mustard.

7. Serve the asparagus spears with the dipping sauce.

37. Crispy Jalapeno Coins

Prep + Cook Time: 15 minutes | Servings: 1-2

Ingredients:

- 2-3 tbsp. coconut flour

- Pinch of garlic powder

- Pinch of onion powder

- Cajun seasoning for an extra kick, optional

- Salt and ground black pepper to taste

- 1 jalapeno, sliced and seeded if desired

- 1 egg, raw, mixed well

- Cooking spray or oil mister

Directions:

1. Make sure the air fryer is preheated to 400-degree F.

2. Thoroughly combine the recipes, except for the egg and jalapeno.

3. Strip the extra water from the jalapeno slices by patting them dry with a paper towel.

4. In the mixture, dip each slice in the egg and wipe it dry. Toss it to coat it. You are required to reapply until it sticks well.

5. In the air fryer, pass the coated jalapeno slices while grouping them into a single plate.

6. For some cooking oil, spray gently.

7. Enable them to cook until the coins are nice and crispy. Owing to the scale of the slices, turning once during the cooking time.

8. Serve hot.

38. Healthy Mediterranean Vegetables

Prep + Cook Time: 30 minutes | Servings: 4

Ingredients:

- 1 large courgette

- 1 green bell pepper

- 1 large parsnip

- 1 medium carrot

- 2 oz. cherry tomatoes

- 6 tbsp. olive oil

- 2 tsp garlic puree

- 1 tsp mixed herbs

- 1 tsp mustard

- 2 tbsp. honey

- Salt and ground black pepper to taste

Directions:

1. Cut up the courgette and the green pepper at the base of the air fryer. Peel and dice the parsnip and the carrot and, though still on the plant, throw in the cherry tomatoes. This brings more spice to the mixture.

2. Cook the mixture for 15 minutes at 360-degree F after drizzling three tablespoons of olive oil.

3. Combine the remaining ingredients in a baking dish appropriate for your air fryer when cooking.

4. From the base of your air fryer, cut the fried vegetables and pass them into the baking dish.

5. Shake well to ensure all portions of the vegetables are coated by the marinade.

6. Cook at 390-degree F for 5 minutes after sprinkling a little extra pepper and salt.

7. Just serve.

Chapter 18: Dessert Recipes

39. Caramel Cheesecake

Prep + Cook Time: 55 minutes | Servings: 8

<u>Ingredients:</u>

- 1 can condensed milk

- 6 digestives

- 2 oz. butter, melted

- ½ lb. caster sugar

- 1 lb. soft cheese

- 1 tbsp. vanilla essence

- 4 large eggs

- 1 tbsp. chocolate, melted

<u>Directions:</u>

1. Place the can of condensed milk in your Instant Pot without the can wrappings getting under the water. Set your Instant Pot to MANUAL, seal, and allow cooking for 40 minutes.

2. Ensure that your air fryer is preheated to 360-degree F

3. Using your hands, apply some flour on the base and sides of the spring form pan to ensure that it does not get sticky.

4. Hammer the digestive biscuits with a rolling pin inside a sandwich bag or its wrappers to form crumbles.

5. Combine the biscuit crumbles and the melted butter inside the spring form pan. Mix well with your hands to ensure it pushes down on the base.

6. Get a clean mixing bowl, and in it, combine the sugar and the soft cheese until you have a nice and soft mixture. For best results, use a hand mixer. Add the vanilla essence and the eggs, and mix well with the mixer. Set aside.

7. Cool the condensed milk when it is done. Then open it up and empty the caramel into the bowl. With the aid of a fork, mix it in before placing the mixture over the biscuit base in the spring form pan.

8. Use your spatula to make it smooth and level.

Allow cooking at 360-degree F for 15 minutes, reduce the heat to 320-degree F and cook for another 10 minutes, and finally cook at 300-degree F for 15 minutes.

9. After cooking, remove from the air fryer and place in the fridge for like 6 hours.

This allows the cake to set before drizzling small amounts of leftover caramel and melted chocolate.

10. Serve.

40. Don't **Go** Heating' the House Gluten-Free Fresh Cherry Crumble

Prep + Cook Time: 1 hour 20 minutes | Servings: 4

Ingredients:

- 1/3 cup butter

- 3 cups pitted cherries

- 10 tbsp. white sugar, divided

- 2 tsp lemon juice

- 1 cup gluten-free all-purpose baking flour

- 1 tsp vanilla powder

- 1 tsp ground nutmeg

- 1 tsp ground cinnamon

Directions:

1. Cube butter and place in freezer until firm, about 15 minutes.

2. Preheat air fryer to 325-degree F.

3. Combine pitted cherries, 2 tablespoons sugar, and lemon juice in a bowl; mix well. Pour cherry mixture into baking dish.

4. Mix flour and 6 tablespoons of sugar in a bowl. Cut in butter using fingers until particles are pea-size. Distribute over cherries and press down lightly.

5. Stir 2 tablespoons sugar, vanilla powder, nutmeg, and cinnamon together in a bowl. Dust sugar topping over the cherries and flour.

6. Bake in the preheated air fryer. Check at 25 minutes; if not yet browned, continue cooking and checking at 5-minute intervals until slightly browned. Close drawer and turn off air fryer. Leave crumble inside for 10 minutes. Remove and allow to cool slightly, about 5 minutes.

CPSIA information can be obtained
at www.ICGtesting.com
Printed in the USA
BVHW042222130421
604819BV00009BA/1229